MW01708770

SEA HORSES

Sea Horses

Karen Mulhallen

Black Moss Press
2007

Library and Archives Canada Cataloguing in Publication

Mulhallen, Karen
Sea horses / Karen Mulhallen.

Poems.
ISBN 978-0-88753-433-1

1. Sable Island (N.S.)--Poetry. I. Title.

PS8576.U414S38 2007 C811'.54 C2007-904113-2

Black Moss Press is published at 2450 Byng Road, Windsor, Ontario, Canada, N8W 3E8. Black Moss books are distributed in Canada and the U.S. by LitDistco. All orders should be directed there. For more information contact Black Moss on its website at www.blackmosspress.com.

Black Moss acknowledges the generous support of the Canada Council for the Arts and the Ontario Arts Council toward its publishing program.

Le Conseil des Arts du Canada | The Canada Council for the Arts

ONTARIO ARTS COUNCIL
CONSEIL DES ARTS DE L'ONTARIO

Sea Horses

… When Neptune's trident tapped the earth,
a horse appeared

(Sic Itus Ad Astra; So the Path to the Stars)

I saw the new moon late yestreen
Wi' the auld moon in her arm

Sir Patrick Spens

… as holy and enchanted
As e'er beneath a waning moon was haunted

Coleridge, *Kubla Khan*

For Zoe Lucas

Sable Island is the exposed portion of an offshore bank on the Scotian Shelf. It is a long, crescent-shaped sandbar, 43 km long and less than 1.5 km wide, located at 44 degrees N, 60 degrees W, 250 km east southeast of Halifax. Circulation over the Scotian Shelf consists of a large cyclonic gyre, a pattern that exists at the surface throughout the year. Gulf Stream eddies seasonally affect water mixing and movement in the area, occasionally delivering more southerly marine animals such as Portuguese-Man-Of-War and, less frequently, the Loggerhead sea turtle, to the island's beaches.On this offshore island a population of feral horses has survived and adapted to life on a sand-bar. During the summer and autumn this sand-bar is cloaked with lush, green vegetation; in winter and early spring its dunes are rather bleak and windswept. Drinking water is available at the numerous fresh water ponds. In addition, the horses dig waterholes in hollows and low areas between the dunes. A brackish lake, Lake Wallace lies just off the south beach. Over the years the size of this lake has diminished. Although early settler accounts talk of sailing parties on Lake Wallace, it is now an irregular salty puddle populated by seal pups. The climate of Sable Island is temperate oceanic and is generally milder than that of mainland Nova Scotia. There are no trees on the island.

(Adapted from texts by Zoe Lucas)

Hippocampus, hippocampos, hippocampi

1. *A sea horse with two forefeet, and a body ending in the tail of a dolphin or fish;*
2. *an enfolding of cerebral cortex into the cavity of a cerebral hemisphere having the shape in cross-section of a sea-horse;*
3. *hippokampos, a seamonster.*

Contents

I

Arrivals/Beginnings

Dream 17
After the Beginning 18
Arrivals 19
Dream Island 20
Sand 21
Sand Dunes 22
Plan A 23
Plan B 24
Tall Tales 25
Threshold 26
Secret 27
Walking 28
Sea Horse 29
Welcome to the Sandbar Hotel 30
Hauntings 31

II

Sable Island

Crusoe on South Beach 35
Secret on the South Beach 36
In The Throb of Silence 37
Net 38
Silk 39
Allure 40
Weather 41
Vertical Man 42
Evening/Morning 44N-60W 43
Horse and Seal 44

Home Thoughts from the North Beach 46
Seal 47
Beach Companions 48
Funeral Prelude 49
Mass 50
Sable Horses 51
ZOE tropes 52
Sea Breeze 56
The Eleventh and Twelfth of August 57
The Fourteenth of August 58
The Fifteenth of August 59
Iphigenia on Sable 60
Last Supper 62
Pathways 63

III
Imprints

Liminal 67
Zenith 68
Passed Noon 69
The Sea Horse 70
Haiku for Wind in Mind 71
Eternity 72
All the Houses That Jack Built 73
Psyche's Tasks 74
Noisescapes, Moonscapes, Dreamscapes 77
Wind 79
Archivists of Mourning 80
Afterword/ Identity 81

IV
Notes

85

I

Arrivals/Beginnings

Dream

This begins with the dream, a dream of wild horses.
This begins with the phrase, dropped casually.
There is an island, a maritime island, island of wild horses.

This is not a dream of the steppes of hither Asia
of the pampas of South America.
This is a dream of Canada.

An island of sand, of lisp and hurl of water, of grasses,
of bird calls, heady with flowers,
Canada.

Somewhere in childhood someone says "an island of wild horses".
Later the yearning grows, like a poem.

So the years pass and the time arrives.
Time to go, time to go
to Sable Island.

After The Beginning

After the beginning, a dream of wild, yearning, hoping, sighing, sending,
after the extraordinary was the banal,

the packing with its modern fabrics, its micro this and that,
its head lamps, its freeze-dried, and I wondered
not if I should, but if I should take all this intrusive paraphernalia.

I hate the sound of Goretex, loathe microfibre
and the smell of rotted vegetables in the refrigerator. Welcome to Sable,
fresh vegetables a mirage, gone by Sunday, no replacements in sight.

Plan A: It's a go, I am in the rear of an airplane forty years old and counting.
The human brain loses 10,000 brain cells a day.
How many cells does this Britten-Norman Islander have left ?

The ocean—How to ken a whale's path, the wake of seals ?

Thinking of the three oceans of Canada, bound by sea and empire—
north, the Arctic, a circumpolar nation:
the polar bear, our totem animal, the arctic fox, and our love, disappearing;
east, the high Atlantic, drama, ice flows, the perfect storm;
west, the fertile Pacific, hydrothermal vents, ghost haunt of the lonely orca Luna.

Clichés, picturesque beauty/ briny deep.

Arrivals

On the mainland was the waiting
and the waiting was with the fog, and the waiting was the fog.

There was no knowing what was ahead, or when.

The main's shore showed its rawness,
city in a landscape of scrub and water.
Everything man-made felt provisional.

Hideous shopping malls, highways,
hopes of families, suburban housing,

human dreams, nature's verities
making for that other shore,
day by day.

Dream Island

I knew it would be a dream,
one moment become the next, time
and space continuous, as image, our life.
The arrival unexpected the day of take-off
even the time-table, arrivals, departures, distances, all askew.

Suddenly airborne, Sean, the pilot, gestures back to me
desperately holding the plane's life raft, I
crane my neck wondering at a whale path,
fin whales, humpback whales, blue whales' tall blow holes hanging,

leading us there to crescent moon of land, sand, green, buff,
small white buildings: what can this be,
such stuff in it, such beings?

Sand

In particular it was the sand, granules composed
of who knows what, all about scale and littoral moment,
some a deep purple full of magnetite
sending off/skewing all electronic resonancing
by the Convair 580, twin engine turbo props
shattering silence, tracking and mapping
surveillance,

and the other moments/particulate
ivory yearning between toes and soft sussuration
as it passes through the hour-glass of the hands
fingers gold and white and the temptation to slip into it,
to slip out of, to reform
in a skin of minute slither
of glitter.

Sand Dunes

shaped by the gyre of wind, fluid, waves,
sand cliffs, sand, sea, gentle undulations,
and risings, up, flat, or ripples, or piles,
always bound to the wind. Crystals of quartz,
fire formed, metamorphic.
Winds direct, turbulent, incomparable velocity
following the clock as it moves
leaping, saltating, creeping.

Plan A

It's a go
to ocean, blue grey of sky
    populous with birds
plane dipping with air currents,
one boat below wakes the sea
smattering of cirrus streamers and alto-cumulus puffs.
  Who is hanging out their laundry on this windy day?
Pasiphae resists the Bull.

Plan B

Descent
is a fall, and a drawing back, falling back into love,
panic, withdraw and bank.

Now land, but pull up,
and land again, go slow now, taxi,
look out, out, you're stuck
in a rut, accelerate, just for a moment:
            Stop,
                  you must be the poet.

Tall Tales

Terns nesting in road bank squall and the first night
cacophony of surf, gulls, sparrows, voices
all the livelong widening blackness, wind become words
conversations in pitch and howl.
 I listen to their voices,
these hauntings, until first light.
What words are these? The Lady of the Ring and Finger,
blood dripping from her finger stump.
 For seventeen years, the Lunatic running his classroom of horses,
"Now, long ears, pay attention, do not eat the grass in school,
you are here to learn".
 As am I. So many misty foolish sorrowing Sable haunters.
We must release these human simulacra, tall tale tellers.
Leave the place to its true elements: birds, horses, sand, seals.

Threshold

Fire alarm/initiation

First morning, bleary at muster point,
night of hauntings, nightgown to first light.

To the south, colony of terns on road.
To the north, a gate of flowers and sea grasses,
hair and bones of a dead foal,
dead sparrow, delicate toothpick legs in air,
white yarrow, white beach petunias,
bright pink portulaca, spots of blue, a yellow sundrop on a cleomé stem,
lush dark green ground cover, spiky grasses, clamour:
my eyes, ears, nostrils, skin reeling senses
in a parliament of fowls.

Secret

To know weather is to know the world,
and I a library cormorant have come here
to know this place. The lisp of sea.
Sand resistant to the water's pleadings, assaults.
To choose to write is to choose the
secret longing/
                    blowing through.

Walking

Walking. Walking toward a spot on horizon.
Spot becomes group, two fuzzy foals, four adults,
horses in the lee of dune, eating, grazing, being.

Water is warm, redolent of seal, sweet silver heart faces,
shimmery grey beingness, harbour seals, popping up
and down, staring, facing, pacing, stalking me.

North beach, water rolls gently in to shore. Sand, a mass of glyphs—
mystery of V shapes, gibbous moon hollows, tractor traces. Sea is green.
Later a fog, and the West Point, no longer visible.

Two hours through soup to home base, and the making of baked apples
in maple syrup. Talk of helicopters, life in the woods,
living in a loin cloth, beef farming, first speech.

Sea Horse

Sea horse of your penis, lying nestled beneath brood
pouch of belly. I recognize you, and remember to
  Construct the Rules for Normal Engagement:
1. Do not say you love him, unless he says he loves you;
2. Do not say you love him, unless he asks if it be so;
3. Say you want him, even when he does not say he wants;
4. Stand always at a distance, but listen for the breath;
5. Incline your head/yourself/but not too close;
6. Observe private spaces.
    Avert one eye from the horse, as it rises.

Welcome to Sandbar Hotel

One hand, four inches; a pony, less than 13 hands.
The line of a poem, the line of the hand; a Sable horse, a sonnet.

Over the mantel of the fireplace in the Sandbar Hotel lounge
hangs a photograph of Sable and Sandy,
removed from their island paradise, and placed in a Wildlife Park, June 1973.
In this picture, signed *P. Spike, October 1974*, the earth is bare,
packed, and dry. In the distance are trees;
in front of them, a running fence. Easy to see

the scene-disturbing contrast to mist-laden, lush, flower-bedecked,
dune-defined, moon-pulled isle, fed by the Gulfstream's seasonal eddies,
persistent cyclonic gyre. Easy to say contravenes the Shipping Act
protecting their souls. Easy to hear mourning.
To this place, we measurers have carried mice, rabbits, rats,
foxes, cows, goats, pigs, oxen, bulls, dogs, cats, horses—none remain
but the horses, and we the temporary record keepers,
from a place east of Eden.

Hauntings

Friday I arrived, flying in over the blue whale's path, its forked flukes
and the oil derrick clearly in view to the west of West Light.

Two men in hats greeted me on the sand, you must be the poet, said one,
as he shook my hand.

In a white clapboard house, I chose a bedroom, arranged belongings,
switched mattresses.

Abetted by departing ham radio operators, I settled in, everything
I could have imagined, then more.

Darkness came, swiftly I was alone in the Sandbar Hotel.

Rhythms take days: a writing space, a meal pattern, walking on the dunes.

That first night they came—there was no warning, the wind blew,
the voices entered.

Air currents from the main in the solitude; remnants of those thrown up on
shore from the briny deep; clingings of the mad abandoned on this perilous isle.

Exhausted, I could not sleep and rode the crest of night, borne by the
talk of the house, its frantic chatter.

II

Sable Island

Crusoe On South Beach

gets picked up by a pack of seals
all the way to Lake Wallace.
    Don't worry, we'll keep you company.
You thought you came here for quiet, solitude, no kidding!
There are forty thousand more where I just popped up,
and we're all headed in the same direction, your direction—
Lake Wallace.
    We don't get to hang out with someone like you very often.
I mean, you're on foot, looking at the waves, nobody else does that around here;
besides we have to check on our babies—they like that brackish overwash,
born there somewhere between sand and water.
    Phaah, off you go.
Sorry we can't tag along, into that sahara of sand over there.
You do it, and we'll meet you at a salty lip.
We have our own way in, and really,
I don't advise you ditch all that stuff you're carrying,
in order to come here with us.
You'll meet a few of our buddies over there in sand-land.
Don't mind their stares, they're like that.
    Toodle-oo-hoo!
Hah-eehou.

*

Call of gulls, sand slips to bubbling foam,
sudden aroma, attar of rotting seal.
Rough the waves, resistant the shore, foam, foam, curl and struggle.
Each curl of green with a silhouette of seal,
translucent as Murano masters make.
    Pups like minnows sliding down sandbanks into sea.
Pure joy of rise and dip,
a seal pup in bliss in a breaking wave.
Line of black sleekness/ in a thrust of sea.

Secret on the South Beach

Two storey building, nestled into dune,
hugged by grasses and thick ground cover.
From its windows seals sunbathe on the lake below.

Once on its cool dark floor, hidden, a couple, runaway,
made love, spoke of meeting again and again,
but they were spotted, found out,
by those spelunking who belong there.

To its east, cut through to the gentle swoosh of north beach,
heady signs of horse trail— flaxen-maned yearling, chestnut, two foals, my six in a row,
my totem band, head to love's caverned house, as I turning descend.

Always aware of the compass, and always disoriented.
Which way is the way, the right, the sinister, and how to choose
the line, the page, the chapter of our lives?
Which book do we belong in, after all?

Black beauty appears, a white diamond on his forehead,
legendary stallion of the broken foot picks his way carefully
through the pond of burning water, dream of wild horses,
off the carousel, into the west.

In The Throb of Silence

Always someone else's words seem right, and the wrong is always the attempt
to find the way alone. The past beats inside me like a second heart.
I try to bury it in the throb of silence, but sometimes it threatens to annihilate me.
Familiar gods take new forms, but maybe it is the simple fact
of you.

Net

The evening I met you in someone else's living room
I wore black lace net stockings, seamed,
a Christmas gift from my mother scarcely three months before,
and I never wore them ever ever again.
Over these years the elastic gave
the waist sagged
and I tossed them this morning to the garbage men
in a truck which traverses both our streets.

Silk

The night I met you there was another man
skin like silk, a writer, generations older.
He pronounced me profound
ignoring how foolish I would become that evening,
or perhaps to be profound is to be the fool.
To refuse to measure, to refuse to calculate,
to simply accept, that this is inevitable,
for as long as it takes.

Allure

I have come here with my notebook, pens and texts
which I devour as the lore of horses has devoured me.
It is a dream of childhood, though mine was bound with the warmth of cows,
barbed wire and cow-plop, its squish between the toes,
the sharp cut of fence on my back.
   An old cutter drawn around the fairgrounds on a snow-packed track.
Elegant Mrs Nesbitt, Effie, so beautiful in her furs
and her horse-drawn sleigh, a being from a book of fairy tales,
not the stern black buggies and clothes and whips of Amish farmers,
or thistles, thorns, swirl of bagpipes and tug of rope,
but the sheer poetry of a mane in the wind, the lure.

Weather

The weather here is squally, strong, also mild.
It is a mirror for my love which, self-reflecting, gets buried
in the daily of each of our lives.
Like scarcely beaten egg whites, small waves
break in listless line over my bare feet,
aliens in this sand welling from the gully just off shore.
A swell emerges from darkness, lifts me up,
as if from that deeper source, the very earth's core,
and I am carried back into that other place
I came here searching for.

Vertical Man

With his glass globe, he measures the heat of the sun
sends a ray to the height of the clouds

strides around space, dunes reaching up.

Horses see light
hear the jingle of machines

which cut the thrust of wind
catch the rain

measure the flow of the spheres.

Mornings, he launches a balloon.
Evenings too, it grows sevenfold

touches the starry canopy
and speaks around the terrestrial globe.

Seals ascend dunes,
clog roadways in winter.

All summer pups sun, squirm, swim
black minnows on dun, in blue, on foam.

Foals drop down, stand up on spindles
soft as eiderdown, sweet as morning dew.

Terns dive angrily, catapult toward the road
where a stranger walks

by nests secreted in walls of sand,
tethered by juniper roots, scented with rose, cranberry-capped.

Evening/Morning
44N-60W/Station Life

Just after eight p.m., sun sets, vertical man does his evening rounds.
Pale blue sky streaked with red. Deeper red to hot pink in the west.
South, a very pale blue, like the blue of your eyes.

A crescent moon appears, mirrors the land below,
thumbnail in its last quarter, as am I.
Red cloud turns to smoke, pinks deepen, grasses darken.
Small white buildings stand out from soft undulations of yellow green grass.

Venus, our star, the star of evening appears, emerges
as upper clouds turn to sooty streaks.
And the lower are red and grey, outlining the radio tower,
the distant buildings, the light house.

Then all is soot.
Night falls.

Toward midnight, a light show on the east lights up the western sky.
So much lightning, the Lady of the Chopped Off Finger returns,
looking again for her ring and talking, talking again, all through the night,
bereft of ring and finger.

Morning rounds, vertical man is wired, checks the gates against those horses.
They love to rub their asses against expensive equipment.
Don't we all, don't we all.

Horse and Seal

Here two beings with the greatest intimacy
profound, silent.
They never touch.

You might call them
horse and seal
if that is your only language.

And horse and seal
they do appear to be
if bodily form deceive not the eye.

Horse wishes to travel;
seal wants to be here forever.

Horse despises islands;
seal has found paradise.

They meet to converse,
talk it over on a dune
overlooking the gentle waves of the north beach.

They meet to discuss differences,
converse from the sand-flats
overlooking the rough breakers of the south.

Horse is lanky, angular; seal is small, smooth.
Horse moves all his joints as he trots.

Seal is quick, moves like grains of sand.
Horse's eyes are the colour of the early morning sky;
so are seal's.

Horse's coat shimmers silver, so does seal's.

Horse and seal travel together
and they travel apart.

Horse contemplates sky, wind,
changing light, planetary spheres,
poetry of line, and filament, and arc,

instruments centuries old
calibrations of wire and rain
hail clouds of cedar wax-wings

on the Fischer-Porter precipitation gauge,
sun-scorch marks on the cardboard strips
of the Campbell-Stokes recorder.

Seal examines minute forms
carcasses of the elemental: bone, flesh,
a dish-shaped nose, a battered wing, a heap of wrack,

a lobster's claw, a turtle's head, a dead dolphin,
a beached whale shark, an eyeless trigger fish
: seals, birds, beetles, horse.

Home Thoughts from the North Beach

Rising up over the green of dunes
from the north, a line of bruised blue mountains,
darker, larger, loomings, gloaming.
Fog rolling in and over
blocking sightings of the green sea.
Then sunlight arrives, dispels
cumulus fluff to the west.
Stratus streamers stretch to the south,
sound of birds rises:

As when you come to a place long anticipated
and know it for the first time.

Seal

Harbour seal, none sweeter,
with a heart-shaped face, small nose, blue eyes.
She is smaller than a grey seal, smaller than horse.
She arrived as a young pup on the beach and just settled in.
Wonders why she didn't know sooner about this place,
short-circuiting those tesky adolescent years,
happiness only a quick trip from shore.
Conservation is her thing,
and she's a dab hand at counting and omelets, and all kinds of sauces.
She whirls around a kitchen like a dervish, and gathers beach debris for mobiles
and her spirit people, stacked in a corner of her dwelling
which grows out of the sand of the north beach near West Point.
Hard to believe a seal would be interested in Michael Jackson,
but she's that kind of seal and he's there alright
among the spirit people propping up a corner near her front door.
She's been here for decades, and at first she would get lost, disoriented.
Once she saw some UFOs, thought they'd come to take her away,
made her confession, her amends for her deeds. and got ready.
But it was just the station lights over the hill.
Now, like Wilda, who melted away
just north of the ponds to the north of the station,
she'll give herself to the island,
be recycled by gulls, terns, beetles, sand.
She'll stay here, she says, subsiding into the earth
like the horses.

Beach Companions

Dead dolphin, dead sea turtle, dead whale shark—
    all day riding with Zoe on the back of her bicycle, roaring on the sand,
as we rise and fall, and Zoe takes us over, up, down, across, around,
as I lean to collect balloons, wedding balloons, birthday balloons,
promotional balloons, sinister balloons, righteous balloons, political balloons,
sexual balloons, motto-less balloons, proverb-bound balloons,
ribbonless balloons, festooned balloons, all for her count.
Persistent beach litter.
                    And the sea creatures whose heads Zoe tries to collect,
                        but her scalpel keeps coming apart.

Funeral Prelude

Cold dune as we cut away at Bress and the mare who has only a number.
It is heavy fog today, unlike two days ago when sweltering,
we could not bear the heat from sand and sky.

I can see some of the station buildings. The horses have subsided near their
companions, human and otherwise. Our restless knives cut and dig and we carry
grey boxes cross dunes down to Zoe's Honda Fourtrax bike.

Bress is deep in the sand, but the one who is only a number is more on the
surface, with the number tag through her eye socket. A smaller beast, her bones
still bound by sinew. Zoe cuts off her tail still intact with its bone.

Mass

Impossible to say
how I feel about gathering for science,
this day, out on a dune off the south beach, collecting skeletons of the two
who died two years ago, Bress and one who is simply a number.

Fog soup in the foggiest and windiest place in eastern Canada.
The station buildings, an impossible to know distance away.

It is cold as we cut back some of the vegetation.
One horse has returned deep into the earth,
up through her bones and flesh the marram grass has grown.

Rest in peace, sweet Bress.
May your spirit rest, as our restless knives cut away
to gather your bones in grey plastic.

On a rise is the next—this more on the surface,
numbered but nameless, sinews binding her small bones.

I am mourning these deaths, the harshness of winter,
as I learn to cut and to gather.
Surely their spirits have fled into the land.
Surely their souls intact here,

as we clamber over the dunes with a second heavy grey box:
Vite, missa est—
    Go, the mass is over.

*

Exode
Off to the beach through persistent litter to gather balloons.
Today the south is rough.
Seals, swift minnows, rush off in the foam surf.
Zoe takes us along the lip in the fog.
Dunes no longer visible.
Veer to the right road station appears.
Incense of rotting poet.

Sable Horses

Since 1738, many breeds have been introduced to the stock. with the result that the horses which remain, through natural selection, tend to resemble North African horses, Barb, with small rounded wide set ears and fine muzzles and thin curved nostrils, mainly Roman noses, although a few have finely dished faces, small round hooves, narrow deep chests, heavy shoulders and short heavy legs.

ZOE tropes

Conversation with ZOE I

If man is to remain on this planet, Sable might be a good model for what is possible. Our footprint here has let the horses be and the vegetation too. The horses are healthy; their coats ungroomed glisten. When they break a leg, a foot, are wounded, they do recover. There is no intervention. I get my DNA samples only from the dead. Trace lineages, keep a watch over them. It's a loss when I lose a stallion or two from a line I am tracing. I could be following a brood mare and a band stallion for twelve years, and one winter, a severe one, I might lose a horse or two, and the lineage trace is broken.

This morning above the wind I hear a Convair 580, twin engine turboprop in the sky. I find out it belongs to the National Research Council and it's part of a joint Canadian and American Defense project collecting geomagnetic observations of Sable.

Months later, by a fresh water sea, I type these words into my computer, from my notebooks in the old dining room on the south shore of another island, facing the water, glimpsed moving through bare tree branches. It is February, winter in Toronto, but above the tide and the waves, I can hear the birds. It is not Sable Island. But it is protected, and it returns me to what I have left behind, even as I enter here.

Conversation with ZOE II

Sable Island is not of such great biological interest as the Galapagos, although people have tried to sell Sable Island as the Canadian Galapagos. However, while Sable Island does not support a community of flora and fauna as rich and unique as that of the Galapagos, there is significant biodiversity here—indeed six species found on Sable are endemics, and there may be additional endemic species found when Sable's invertebrate fauna is studied in more detail.

There are some introduced plant species surviving on Sable (and mostly thriving only in areas of human activities, near buildings), but the horses are the only introduced/feral wildlife. The nesting seabirds, shorebirds and sparrows are all indigenous—not introduced—likewise the seals, the invertebrates (spiders, beetles, bugs, bees, dragonflies, and so on) and the fish in the ponds.

Maritime Canada has many ecologically precious areas that are currently more threatened than Sable Island, but Sable Island's fragile environment's continuance and stability depends on the maintenance of Environment Canada's Sable Island Station which protects the island and monitors its life.

Each day the horses are getting closer, taking me over, or letting me in. Only a moment ago, for the first time just beyond my writing desk, at the fence, a band appeared. A yearling, a foal, a flaxen-maned golden palomino, a pure rusty chestnut, and a bay.

Conversation with ZOE III

This is the only nesting ground for the Ipswich Sparrow in the world. Seventeen kinds of birds nest here, but more than 350 species have been sighted. Because of the island's location, and the wild weather, they get blown about over the sea and, off course, flutter down on this sand bar.

In the autumn, birds come and go—the gem-like Warblers flit in the vegetation and occasionally inside buildings. Whimbrels are feeding in the heathlands, and soaring over the dunes with their wind-chime calls. Ruddy Turnstones are feasting on bugs, beetles, flies and maggots, that are seething in and around the stinky corpses of seals on the beach. For a Turnstone, the aroma of rotting seal means there's a feast available (a sort of church supper for shorebirds).

One fall day I saw four eastern Phoebes, also Western and Scarlet Tanagers and a Marsh Wren. White Crowned Sparrows and White-Throated Sparrows. There was a Kestrel happily snacking on the sparrows.

June brought a White-winged Dove, and the discovery of the corpse of a Magnificent Frigate bird.

My own routine is now set. I wake each day before 6 a.m., then doze-dream until just before eight, listen to the surf, the wind, the birds. Hit the button for coffee, set up the night before. I prepare breakfast, and after the first cup of coffee, make a light lunch for Zoe and myself. Then I take to my sun porch to write and to read. My desk is set looking toward the north and the west and I can see the fence line of the compound beyond which a small family of five horses likes to forage in the grass. Between me and the fence is Downtown Sable Island, research buildings for the atmospheric monitoring equipment, and the geomagnetic sensors, and the windsock tower. Station Manager Gerry Forbes's two-storey white clapboard house, the garage where the balloons and radiosondes are released twice a day, I can see the set of the boardwalk in the grass leading toward my own family of horses, and the lens of fresh rain water with grasses poking through it, the result of Thursday's downpour. It's their grass stew. Hors d'oeuvres. Horse delight.

Conversation with ZOE IV

When I first came here, I had trouble figuring out which was where. One evening I had been out on the beach checking on sea birds, and it had gotten dark, as I came up over the dunes from the north beach I saw lights and I thought a UFO had landed. I was ready to go and make amends and be taken.

The horses work and live in bands but individuals do migrate.
Especially the stallions and occasionally the yearlings.
Families are not necessarily blood-related, but the mares tend to stick with their foals.
Males prance and run together as aggression. Sometimes rear legs rise to kick.

People often ask where the horses get their drinking water.
Many horses dig for water in all seasons, and never visit a pond.
Others drink from ponds or dig for water depending on the time of year,
and some, perhaps about 20% of the population, drink from the freshwater ponds year round.

Today several foals on the dunes off the north beach by West Point. Two of them come to me. One is a real little punkinhead, his flaxen bushy mane sticking up above his rusty birth coat still shaggy on its back and head.

Sea Breeze

Today was like no other day, helicopter fracturing the air,
drowning the squawking of the tern colony, the call of gulls and wind.

A large grey metal dragonfly hovered over our small world,
seeming to threaten its fragile frame buildings.
But it landed on its own pad, and out of it scurried seven figures
dressed in camouflage clothing, heading for the garage near the main road
to spend the day wrapping smoke flares, beach litter collected over time.

The flares still had remnants of phosphorous and magnesium dioxide
and the Canadian army had arrived to blow up the flares,
wrapping each in C-4 and then transporting them
down to the east end of south beach to detonate.

While some of the crew wrap in the garage,
the chopper leaves for the nearby oil rig to refuel.

The camouflage flight crew invades the house I share with the Lady with the
Chopped Off Finger. Hours elapse. The television blares near my writing space.
The sound of foreign voices, their restlessness, the clicking of billiard balls.

The sun declines, almost time for me to head off to meet it.

Finally from the south beach the wagon returns as darkness drops.
I climb a dune to look toward the falling light and the light foamy edge of the sea.

A co-pilot appears, a big man, charming, skin the colour of dunes at twilight.
He looks with me toward the sea, his nostrils twitching,
heady smell of grasses, wild rose and bay.

The chopper begins its whirl, the other six hurry from house and garage.
All swagger aboard.

The Eleventh and Twelfth of August

Sunset. Fog off the land rises in bands, radiation mist. Behind it is the sky's glow in grey and red horizontal stripes. Beneath them an infinite darkness. Against this, behind the rising mist from the land, stand the white clapboard frames of the station buildings, and in particular the station manager's simple two-storey east-coast style dwelling.

Morning and I go to Zoe's camp, as two men arrive by the old Britten-Norman Islander plane to service the fire extinguishers. Zoe and I see and hear nine passes of a Canadian military plane taking readings for developing maps which will establish a magnetic field for a joint Canadian-American military defense project. If there were submarines offshore, they would be detected with the established magnetic field. And Sable Island too has its own magnetic field, black sand, magnetite, which will show up on the chart, complicating simple readings. Easy to forget, in this place, the world of NORAD and the web of alliances and treaties and defenses.

In the middle of a pond stands a shimmering black stallion, dipping his head in and out. He is feeding on pond grass, horse stew.

Nearby, on the soft green grassy bank, grazes a new dark bay foal only a few days old. Also hovering nearby are palomino and chestnut and bay mares. A stable little family with two stallions.

The Fourteenth Of August
Sunday Visit

Evening and Paul arrives with a bottle of port for a visit. He tells me he did not begin to speak until he was seven years of age. He grew up in Guernsey in a protected pastoral idyllic world, high bracken all around the deep valley in which the family farm was located, When he was just eleven, his father died of a heart attack. His mother remarried, and his step-father James is his best friend. James and his mother decided to emigrate from Guernsey to Nova Scotia. Guernsey people are emigrators. You find them everywhere. Take Sarnia, Ontario. Sarnia was the original Roman word for Guernsey. Jersey too is Guernsey. Guernsey is an English channel island known for banking and the pastoral. Paul believes empires rise and decline. He believes in the "force" as well, for who can say who created the life-lines between Stonehenge and the chalk horse. England, its barrows and fens, dense, mysterious, layered places. Who would disagree?

When Paul leaves, I think about the stories he has told me about himself. For a year he lived in a helicopter hangar. He also lived in the woods for a year, wearing only a loin cloth and snaring rabbits for food. At the age of fourteen he had his own beef cattle farm which he sold when he was seventeen, just as the market was falling.

There are many versions of each of us, and Paul is a man who sees the world as in terrible shape, which of us does not, who worries about the possibility of Apocalypse, who thinks perhaps Sable Island would be the best place to live beyond the conflagration, who also thinks of emigrating to Australia. And so, as I am heading upstairs to bed, I remember Margaret Atwood's second dystopia, *Oryx and Crake*, a post-apocalyptic novel set in Australia. And I realize again that Percy Shelley's *Defense of Poetry* is right when Shelley argues that poets are the unacknowledged legislators of the world. It is the poets—artists of all kinds—who see the shadows which futurity casts upon the present. *Oryx and Crake*!

The Fifteenth of August

This evening before sunset I set out to visit my favourite little family, two mares, two foals and a yearling who hang around, just west and north of the compound on the dunes, in the valleys, and near the ponds. In fact in this area is the island's only lily pond, with its red-breasted mergansers and the world's only fresh-water sponges.

Over the rise comes a palomino yearling with a blaze of white on her forehead and a long silken white mane. She is very gold in the evening light, and even more golden against the characteristic chestnut Sable horses with their ruddy coats. My golden girl is intent on one of the foals and leaves her mother on a grassy hill over the dune to descend into the valley to nuzzle the foal.

I love the curiosity of these beings, their sweet investigations of one another. I sit on the far hill watching as the light scatters from their shoulders, and mine, and then the horses decide that I too must be visited, and they begin to pick their way up the steep incline toward me.

Iphigenia on Sable

I gaze at the foreshore of my little island kingdom. It is rank wilderness, all trees and rocks with birds swinging on the off-shore breezes. As for the Great River of Canada, I cannot see the other side of its huge mouth. It looks and acts like a sea or the ocean, grey waves slopping against the rocks, tides rushing in and out, horizon like the curve of a dirty eggshell. Words that come to mind: desolate, dreary, deserved, dreadful, drafty….I say a prayer, then notice a brilliant white bird with a yellow beak and black tips on its wings gliding on the air just feet from where I sit….I know I shall die upon this alien shore, this coastline of mystery, this place called Canada….The smell of the new land is fresh, almost no smell at all, a new world.

Douglas Glover, *Elle* (Goose Lane Editions, 2003)

North cut west to the West Spit. The road is bumpy and then bumpier, the horses sleek and the largest bands come and go. Zoe finds a huge lobster claw—must have come off a forty-pounder. Then a trigger fish missing its eyes, plop into the bike's basket and we lunch on the spit and I fall down an incline into the surf, elbow my way back up to Zoe. We talk above the roar, or beneath it, then off again heading east on the south beach.

At each end of Sable, near the spits, the junctures of north and south beach, are sandcastles, Aztec or Inca temples of towering sand. How tall are these hoodoos at the point? And the vegetation too is thick, a lush carpet. Zoe says it has grown considerably on the west over what was once bare sand, and now the horse herds of the west are in the best shape of all the 50 or 60 herds.

Back on the bike and a wild acceleration, bumps, ascents, descents, gathers, and then a great push of acceleration and we pass up a sandy road to an encampment.

Flags. banners. driftwood. hard-hats. aerosol cans. bones. This is Zoe's laboratory/studio. A fiberglass tube, segmented like a caterpillar, snugged into the sand, on the south west of the island, deep in a dune.

There is shelter here, privacy, a dedicated life.

Zoe's encampment, so like that of Marguerite de la Roche in *Elle*. Another era, another temperament, another life rhythm. Zoe, the scientist; Marguerite, the hoyden. And yet Marguerite's capacity to create and embrace from the ground up, with her pelts, her bones, her dog, her polar bear skin. Sable Island and an island in the St Lawrence River—not so far apart after all. Life affirming fortitude.

Last Supper

This evening we dine communally. We are all a little quiet, perhaps even tense. Hurricane Katrina is moving north, and the air is charged with warning. One speaks to his special relationship with a gander. Another seems to feel the seals deliberately impede his vehicle in winter, getting in through the compound fences, impossible to get around. Pupping is over and they are on the move. The third is very quiet. I am worried about leaving, not ready, and yet there are hurricane warnings. Leave now, or remain until the end…

I have spent part of the day at Zoe's camp, reading *The Nymph and the Lamp*, by Thomas Raddall. I am seated on her indoor sofa reading by moonlight, her LED reading light someone sent her from Ontario. As usual, we eat fruit, some sandwiches, and she makes us chai tea.

There is also an outdoor sofa—a heap of floats she has gathered from the beaches. Rolling around on them, she demonstrates how comfortable they are, how they conform to the body. Zoe's easy smile and laugh. Her delight.

Zoe's bone mobiles, skeletal Calders of Sable Island, her spirit people, balloon ribbon-haired sticks with floats for heads.

Above Zoe's desk is a wall of skulls, all museum-labeled.

Pathways

Stick only to the pathways, I was told. Follow the horses. And yet, there is nowhere without pathways, a mapping by hooves and inclination and identity.

Up this last morning at dawn, after a quick coffee I head west and north at first light to pick up the series of fresh water ponds. There can be no leaving without leave-taking. Somewhere over there is my little punkinhead. Somewhere near the Bren Gun Carrier and the sweet system of ponds, with its blowouts to the north beach and the rising sun.

I have seen herons fishing for Stickleback in the ponds and the lily pond with its freshwater sponges and flocks of red-breasted mergansers floating by. Who knows how long they have been there. It has not been possible for me not to love you, try how I might. It is simply so, but you are a danger for me, a drug, a whirlpool, a maelstrom.
Shoals of shouldn't.

Last night the sunset told of departure. Cumulus of shocking pink cotton candy set everything against it, dunes against the dark green of the ground cover became pink and pinker. Across the roar of wind and tide, a bird winged its way high up on the eddies of air. Psychedelic massing against the deepening blue. I am looking to the east whence my comforts might increase, my heart is moving west, home to you.

III

Imprints

Liminal

She seemed to slip away out of the very confines of life itself, out of her human skin, out of that house; she was *floating in some airy region where forms and shapes and sounds had been left behind—had changed into something else.*

Melodies, waves, rhythms, washing over me,
as the wind howls through the dunes—
plus jamais, plus jamais
encore j'ai mon coeur
j'ai mon coeur, j'ai mon coeur
j'ai ton coeur, j'ai ton coeur
never again, never again,
mais encore, mais encore
I have my heart, you have my heart
I have my heart, tu as mon coeur
mon coeur/
corage.

Zenith

Spelling the horses' tracks, numbering the curves and bends of grass,
I head to north beach through spears of green and flowers.

Grass ripples, changes colour as it moves.
Spell and sound of sea, deep blue. Sand and small foam at shore.

I am high on a dune. To my south, the station compound,
men move constantly between buildings.

Grass. Flowers. Dunes. Sand. Beach. Breakers. Water. Seals. Horses.
I am high, but I can not touch the sky.

Under my white hat, I doze on a bank of juniper, bay, wild roses, cranberry.
Caught in the spell of the spelling of it all, so many sibilants.

North, a solitary seal in the sea.
East, beach bound, a pack of harbour seals.

Soul begins to climb, up into azure heights,
buoyed by surf, scents, and the yipping of seals.

Passed Noon

Desperate for water and the path home
    (Take the love, and put it in a box)
I search the beach for traces
    (Keep the lid on)
Here a track, there a hoof, here a flipper's sweep
    (Take the love, and plant it in a garden)
Passed my expiry date, I must sit down, and check the shore for juncture
    (Watch the seepage)
Take a slow slide into the surf
    (Take the love, and give it to another)
Cool, cool touch of the long absent lover
    (It returns)
The shark infested sea.

The Sea Horse

preoccupies me
its sweet curve at the edge of the crook of your loins and your thigh
enfolded like the hippocampus, sea monster/
sea horse, no need to lift up to aggression,
so easily it can be asked to dance;
in repose it is simply at rest,
and age carries that tranquility
in the most sweet form:

I would not give back these twenty years for anything—
not true, I would give them back
to have had them with you,
to have had the dance of years
the brain's cortical enfoldings
with you, but nothing else.

Haiku for Wind in Mind

and the sweet sun spills
outward dividing shadow
camera and colt.

Eternity

She felt that her senses were no longer available, no longer to be trusted. She had slid away somewhere, where human existence and human contact meant nothing at all.

She had been drawn to him, as if by a magnet strong enough to move a great ship of prejudices and clichés *en masse* across the deep.

Airy and light as it now was, her soul had been liberated in some secret way from all that clogged and burdened it.

As if the immense peace of a summer night had turned into a trireme of deliverance carrying the liberated to heaven.

One of her last *thoughts was of the vast tracts of unknown country that every human consciousness includes in its scope.*

A far extending continent, *each with its own sky, its own land and water, its own strange blowing winds.*

The horses' manes, the winds, the grasses, the surf
at once.

All the Houses That Jack Built (1553-2007)

Long before the horses there were cattle, pigs, foxes. Portuguese fishermen using the island as a fishing station landed cattle and pigs to serve as a source of fresh meat. French colonists in 1598 mention cattle, but no pigs. In 1663, John Rose of Boston reports cattle, and red and black foxes, but by 1676 no cattle, only foxes. In 1738, Andrew LeMercier of Boston established his settlement and brought pigs, sheep, and cattle, as well as horses. By 1776, only horses remained. In 1802, cattle, sheep, rabbits and pigs were again brought to the island. Pigs ran wild and began to eat the bodies of shipwreck victims. In 1803, rats and mice were troublesome, so cats were imported. The cats ate all the rabbits but became so numerous and so wild that dogs and men with shotguns killed them. In 1809, rabbits were again introduced, but this time they were killed off by snowy owls. In 1814, a severe winter killed the pigs. In 1844, pigs were again kept, but kept well penned. Sheep were never established, but English rabbits took to the place. In 1850, the lighthouse keepers noted that the island was overrun with rabbits and rats. Finally, the owls and the rats killed the rabbits. Again, rabbits were introduced in 1882, and in 1889 seven cats were sent from Halifax to control them. They were joined by 30 more cats in 1890. That winter, while the cats were getting fat on the rabbits, seven foxes were set loose to control the cats. In one season, the foxes ate all the cats and all the rabbits. When it became clear that the foxes were endangering the bird-life of the island, in 1897, the foxes were hunted and shot.

And so ends the tale of the animals of Sable Island, except of course for the horses, and you, and me.

Psyche's Tasks

<u>Flowers</u>/

Primrose, yellow.
Beach pea, purplish blue.
Wild rose, pink.
Bay.
Blue-eyed grass.
Blue flag iris.
Cranberry.
Yellow lilies.
Round red-haired sundew.
Juniper.
Strawberry.
Blueberry.
Heather—east end on the dune.
Marram grass.
White yarrow.
Everlasting, small white flowers.
Thistle, soft.
A bunch of yews near one of the station buildings.

<u>Horses</u>/

All night the words arrive like horses.

Rituals:
Stealing one another's mares and foals.
Being alone.
Eating.
Running.
Prancing.
Nuzzling.
Licking.
Nipping.
Love Bites.
Head over other's shoulder.
Sniffing.

Kicking.
Standing.
Mane tossing.
Flaring nostrils.
Curiosity.
Coming to me.
Staring, staring.
Alone, in twos, in threes.
Approaching.

Where seen:
Anywhere outside the compound gates,
but most in the tall grasses on the dunes,
in the valleys
in the creases/ on the flanks of the sand and by ponds.

Where perceived:
Hemlines, seams
in droppings on horse trails,
in footprints on beaches,
in grasses parted for trails everywhere.

<u>Sonorities/</u>

Petrels.
Terns.
Peregrines.
Sandpipers.
Gulls.
Sparrows.
Waves.
Equipment.
Wind.
Surf.

Sea Dunes/

The dunes writhe like folds in a slowly shaken blanket.

The green wet pastures by the sea:
Blackberry.
Blueberry.
Cranberry.
Strawberry.
Blue asters with yellow centres.
Purple clover.

The green fields of the sea.

And what if all this should turn into a book, a story, and never turn back?

Noisescapes, Moonscapes, Dreamscapes

Roar of wind, pound of surf, chirp of birds, buzz of flies,
drilling at the edge of the abyss, humming of equipment—
        where has silence fled?

Dream I/New Moon

Belize, and we are walking toward the mangrove swamp, nests of manatees.
Already I am sick with the absence of you, the coming separation.

Two weeks to enter the jungle of the other, lost
I tap my cane, no guide appears.

Dream II/Waxing Crescent

Toronto, I am in the east end, looking for a home,
then on Toronto Island.

The sound of a flute—a dog's head on a turntable
urging the music on, and on.

Dream III/Half Moon

A man without legs.
A house denuded of furniture.

My dog in a box to the vet.
Play on, play on

DREAM IV/Gibbous Moon

Humped back moon, nearly full, through the horizontal of black rocks
nestles into a grey sky, band of blue rising through the lower branches,
what a convex hum is here where silence has fled.

Now on the move into Castle Hill,
    but the house is way too narrow.

How to arrange books, staircase, our living?

A staircase of glass, a fireplace reaching toward the sky,
opening rooms up, up to roof beams.

There is nervousnesss, shivering, trembling at dislocation,
and then calm.

DREAM V/ Full Moon

A herd of wild horses runs through a pond of burning water.

DREAM VI/Gibbous Moon

DREAM VII/Last Quarter, Half Moon

DREAM VIII/Waning Crescent

Tonight the dreams emerge in rapid sequence through a frame of black branches and rocks near dawn.

I am in the east of the city where the land falls into the lake searching for a house of the heart.

I come to a small street hidden away above a landscape of water and pearls.

At last, a dwelling and a park. With water and maps, I return to base and to family, as the rain depends.

Wind

on the grass/
my fingers on these keys.

I have come to the place where what I desire
is not what others desire.
I have not yet reached the place where I know this instinctively,
but it is now part of my deep knowledge of myself
   and of my relation to the world.

Some Sable horses do not drink from the freshwater ponds.
They dig their own holes for their water.

Archivists of Mourning

Do the mares mourn when their foals die?
Hard to answer.
For a while they stick around,
keep coming back, nosing the dead foal.
Then they move away, go on.

Once something strange happened.
My friend Lisa was here,
and there was a mare who had foaled
and the foal was not in good shape, didn't seem to be doing well.

I thought we should go and check on it.

As we approached, the mare was a little way off, grazing.
She saw us and began to move a little toward us, and a little over.
All the while she was looking at us.
Then she stopped and looked down.

We came up, and there was her dead foal.
We stood there together.
She would look at me, look at it.

Perhaps she hoped you might do something,
not knowing you are just the archivist

Afterword/ Identity

I would like to believe that an island is not the main.
I would like to believe that to celebrate an island is to celebrate that place alone.
But we carry within us so many mains, so many islands.
They break through, and they demand we see them all at once.

In my life, I have been privileged to follow my nose,
and to explore the mains and the horses of the sea,
and to celebrate the uniqueness of this island, Sable Island,
and of the mains, and of the world of the horses of the sea.

IV

Notes

After I returned from Sable Island in the summer of 2005, I read the journals of the first superintendent of the Sable Island Humane Society, the Nova Scotia government's attempt to establish a life-saving mission on the island. *The Sable Island Journals* of James Rainstorpe Morris cover only four years of his nine years on the island, and they tell, as might be expected, of the harshness of the physical environment, and of the almost futile attempts to farm the sand dunes, and capture for work and for food the wild horses. Resistant, and unbelieving after back breaking labour, Morris watched the inexorable failure of his crops, and the dying of the wild horses in his care, as well as many of his own domestic animals, despite his best efforts.

He was more successful in the human lives he saved, and the salvage he preserved from shipwrecks. It was his descriptions of the physical landscape that most took my attention, although I grieved for the wild horses, and his corralling, and eating of them. In four years of daily entries, he only once describes the island as beautiful. *Squally* is his most common adjective, followed by *dark*, *thick*, *rainy*, *foggy*, *gloomy*. In fact, he comments that in all his travels he has never known worse weather. And as the weather is judged to be almost constantly unseasonable, he is led to remark: "I suppose the astronomers have made a wrong calculation in Revolutions, or in the points of the Ecliptic." Although science has made an error, Morris continues with a resigned "Hope is Pilot, and Patience has the helm."

These are the journals of a good man, hard-working, focused, widely talented at organizing, navigating, building, and all manner of other work, but they sent me back to my own "home movie", made while I was on the island with an untried new camera, and I now stared at the extraordinary beauty of the place on each of my amateur frames. There was no effort in my pictures, a simple point and click. And the horses, once captured, as Morris himself allows, were gentle and easy to direct. They simply, I would suspect, died of broken hearts.

Although human settlement on Sable Island has taken many shapes, including its use as a dumping ground for "lunatics" from the mainland, since 1961, the delicate ecosystem and the superb inhabitants of Sable Island have been protected by Canada's Shipping Act. Sable Island is an earthly Paradise, hundreds and hundreds of kinds of plants and birds and insects, and horses, and thousands of seals find safe haven here. Many of these are unique to this habitat. The Island is a centre for wide-ranging environmental research, for pollution, radiation, currrents, and one of only 30 places in Canada where each day at 8:15 a.m. and 8:15 p.m. (11:15 and 23:15 Greenwich Mean Time), a radiosonde weather balloon is sent off to the clouds to provide all of us, in concert with 800 sites worldwide, with a picture of the Earth and its atmospheric conditions.

* * *

There are enormous debts for the making of this book set in a remote place. I must thank the Ontario Arts Council for a Writers' Reserve Grant through Black Moss Press, which helped defray the expenses of my initial journey to Sable Island. And to Gerry Forbes of Environment Canada, the Manager of Operations at Sable Island, who facilitated all my research, many thanks. My brother Steven Naylor and my sister-in-law Pam Ritchie tended me, fed me and encouraged me as we waited onshore for the fog to lift. And Zoe Lucas, biologist, miniaturist, historian, passionate student of the precious landscape of Sable Island, brought me close to the land and its beings.

Some of the writing of this book was encouraged by a stay on Toronto Island at Gibraltar Point Centre for the Arts. I am grateful to the City of Toronto and Toronto Artscape for its support for artists, and its idyllic retreat on the archipelago in the harbour of the city of Toronto.

The description of the horses of Sable Island on page 51 is based on Barbara Christie, *The Horses of Sable Island* (1980), as quoted in Zoe Lucas, "Sable island Horses', *AMBC News* (July 1990)

Moments of two poems in the Imprints section, "Liminal" (page 67) and "Eternity" (page 72) are a redaction of phrases in John Cowper Powys, *Wolf Solent*, 1929 (New York: Penguin Books, 1982), pages 282-283.

Grateful acknowledgement is made as well to four readers who helped me understand the motion of the waves in my early drafts of *Sea Horses*: Brian Fawcett, Leslie Hall Pinder, Virgil Burnett, and Zoe Lucas.

For centuries, Sable Island has been a subject of fascination. Of the many who have studied Sable Island, some have lived there, some have visited. My debt to their texts is as various as the changeable maritime weather.

* * *

Armstrong, Bruce. Sable Island. (1981) Foreword by Thomas Raddall. (Halifax: Formac Publishing, 1987) 210 pp.

Campbell, Lyall. Sable Island, Fatal and Fertile Crescent. (Windsor, Nova Scotia: Lancelot Press, 1974) 104 pp.

Campbell, Lyall. Sable Island Shipwrecks, Disaster and Survival at the North Atlantic Graveyard. (Halifax: Nimbus Publishing, 1994) 200 pp.

Daunant, Denys Colomb. Le Songe de Chevaux Sauvages. (France, 1960) 11 minutes

De Villiers, Marq and Sheila Hirtle. A Dune Adrift, The Strange Origins and Curious History of Sable Island. (Toronto: McClelland and Stewart, 2004) 276 pp.

Keough, Pat and Rosemarie. Wild and Beautiful Sable Island, Seals, Wild Horses and Shipwrecks, Nova Scotia, Canada. (Fulford Harbour B.C.: Nahanni Productions, 1993) 96 pp.

Lucas, Zoe. "The Feral Horses of Sable Island", pp. 1-10 in The American Minor Breeds Conservancy News, Volume 7, number 5 (July-August, 1990)

Lucas, Zoe."Monitoring Persistent Litter in the Marine Environment on Sable island, Nova Scotia.", pp. 192-199 in Marine Pollution Bulletin, Volume 24, number 4 (1992)

Lucas, Zoe. Green Horse Society <www.greenhorsesociety.com>

Morris, James Rainstorpe. Superintendent. Sable Island Journals, 1801-1804. Transcribed by Rosalee Stilwell. (Halifax: Sable Island Preservation Trust, 2001) 168 pp.

Raddall, Thomas H. The Nymph and the Lamp. (950) (Toronto: McClelland and Stewart, 1963) 334 pp.

Wright, Barry, The Fauna of Sable Island. Curatorial Report Number 68. (Halifax: Nova Scotia Museum, 1989) 93 pp.

About the Author

To use terms drawn from her other collections, which book by book seem to be forming a luminous but tough-minded poetic autobiography, 'modern love' is shadowed by 'modern life' just as the life-giving island is threatened by an era of 'acid rain.'

— *Sam Solecki*

The author of nine books of poetry, travel and memoir, Karen Mulhallen is the award-winning editor of *Descant* magazine. She teaches at Ryerson University in Toronto and is working on a new book about the conjunction of art and science in Europe in the late eighteenth century.